COCO CHANEL
AND
CHANEL

DAVID BOND

Queen of twentieth century fashion

Coco Chanel has been acclaimed as the most important fashion innovator in the twentieth century. Her interpretation of "fashion" was a totally new concept for a new century – she designed clothes that were easy to wear, flattering, and timeless. She was the first designer to create and market a perfume that did not smell only of flowers. She also made Chanel accessories – rows of pearls, fake brooches, and quilted purses – part of the fashion industry.

Chanel sold a style of dress more than a fashion. She was the perfect model for her fashion house – slim, lithe, and active and she was the first designer to let that style reach women of all different walks of life. The Chanel suit has been copied more than any other couturier garment and at all different price levels.

Her style was as revolutionary as the times she lived through from the twenties to the seventies; it mirrored the changes, especially women's growing freedom. "I set fashions," she said, "precisely because I went out, because I was the first woman to live fully the life of her times." Chanel achieved internationally wider and longer-lasting fame than any other figure in fashion history.

The Chanel concept evolved and adapted with Coco's canny ability to judge the public's mood. She was recognized as a shrewd business executive and inventive designer as early as mid-1910. She then achieved fame and success during the 1920s and 1930s and then again from the late 1950s to the early 1970s.

After Coco's death in 1971, the "Chanel Look" continued into the 1990s and Chanel merchandise became better known and more widely available than ever before.

Opposite: Coco Chanel in 1929, aged forty-six. By this time, Chanel was an established, high-profile fashion company with Coco firmly leading the business with her revolutionary, casual, easy-fitting style.

Below: The classic Chanel suit from 1964. This design was based on a much earlier one, but has lasted through fashion trends. The basic design of a short-braided cardigan jacket became one of the most copied styles in the fashion world.

Fashion before Chanel

In the 1900s, fashionable women dressed in a very fussy, over-feminine, impractical way. The style of their clothes made it difficult to lead busy domestic or business lives. Fashions were created for women with maids and a leisured, society lifestyle. There

"Two of the many remarkable changes which differentiate the twentieth century from all previous centuries are in transport and in the appearance of women . . . . By the mid-1920s women enjoyed a freedom undreamed of just fifteen years before."
Colin McDowell,
from McDowell's Directory of Twentieth Century Fashion.

was no mass production, and fashion was designed for a rich and formal social life, not like the street fashions of today. At this time, most women still had their clothes individually made by tailors, dressmakers, milliners, and shoemakers – it was a time-consuming process that required several fittings for alterations to be made.

Women's figures traditionally followed an "s" shaped silhouette. Hair was piled on top of the head, large elaborate hats sat on top, trimmed with ribbons, lace, feathers, flowers, and artificial fruit – sometimes all on the same hat! Necks looked long and slender with high collars and waists were pulled into almost unbearable tightness with boned and laced corsets.

Many styles fitted closely over the hips and then flared out from the thighs, to flounce wide and trail on the ground. Women wore a great many garments to complete even one outfit – confining corsets, long underwear, slips, and several petticoats – all intricately made in cotton, lace, or silk and decorated by hand with tucks, pleats, fabric inserts, or embroidery.

The dresses worn over all these undergarments were even more elaborate. Shoulder cape effects in lace or frilled materials were often added and many dresses had extra layers of fabric forming over-sleeves and over-skirts. Gloves were always worn when going out and many hats had face veils. Coco Chanel was to change all this.

Wind of change

In 1908 a Paris designer named Paul Poiret began to challenge the fashion establishment and claimed to free women from the tyranny of the corset. His designs showed the full length and shape of women's legs – a fashion that had not been seen for a hundred years. His clothes were theatrical, sometimes almost costume-like, and they were often thought outrageously unconventional.

His controversial ideas, however, had a strong influence on young, style-conscious women whose lifestyles began to change noticeably after World War I. With the expansion of towns and cities came busier social lives, public transportation improved making people more mobile and many more women could drive cars. "Women drive cars nowadays and this you cannot do with crinoline skirts," Coco remarked. Active sports were enjoyed by women as part of their new found freedom. Also, new, energetic Ragtime dance crazes, such as the Grizzly

Bear, the Bunny Hug, and Turkey Trot, all caught the imagination of the young. Coco saw such changes as an opportunity to put sports and leisure wear into the mainstream world of fashion.

It was clear, then, that the pace of social and technological change was ever-quickening. The resulting demand for more practical clothes provided a unique opportunity for young designers like Coco Chanel who were full of new ideas for the future of fashion.

From rags to riches

Christened Gabrielle Chanel, Coco was born on August 19, 1883, in Saumur, a cavalry garrison town on the Loire River in France. She was a strong, determined character, bright and eager to succeed.

The details of Coco's origins are partly shrouded in mystery. Many differing versions of her life have been given. Chanel was known to alter and contradict her own reminiscences. She even offered varying stories about how her famous nickname "Coco" originated. She was known to say that it had

Above: These fashion victims of the late nineteenth century needed a sense of fun to try skipping in their hats, bustles, and long skirts.

Opposite: Generations of women wore these uncomfortable, figure-constraining, whalebone corsets to exaggerate the curves of the female form.

9

MAISON de MODÈLES

MODÈLES de PREMIÈRES MAISONS

MODÈLES RICHES PROVENANT DES GRANDS COUTURIERS

Above: The Paris that Coco came to in 1909 when she first started making hats in a friend's apartment. She enjoyed mixing with artists and members of high society. She gave them all something to talk about with her own style and new designs.

Opposite: The first signs of Coco Chanel breaking away from the stiffness of corsets with softer, more flowing fabrics, and a more loosely fitting design.

started as her father's affectionate pet name, or that it had been first used by young officers competing for her attention when she was in her late teens, or that it was from a song that she had performed on stage.

Most of the accounts of her early life indicate that she had a deprived childhood. Her father, Albert Chanel, was reputed to have come from a tough, peasant background near Nîmes, in Provence, in France. He had great charm and dark, Mediterranean good looks that Coco inherited. He was often absent from his family, as he worked as a commercial salesman from market stalls in country towns. Coco had two brothers and two sisters, none of whom had her drive and spirit. Her mother, Jeanne Devolle, strove desperately to care for and keep the family together, but died when Coco was twelve years old.

After her mother's death, the family was split up and Coco spent several bleak years in a convent orphanage in Aubazine. At seventeen she went to another garrison town, Moulins, where she attended another convent with her aunt of the same age, Adrienne. The young, impressionable Coco learned self-discipline, good manners, neat housekeeping, and through a fear of being poor again, a careful approach to money.

Through hard personal experience in the orphanage she also learned the importance of immaculate sewing and she later demanded the same from her own work force. At eighteen Coco and Adrienne went to work as assistant seamstresses in a shop in Moulins.

Forming a style

The Chanel fashion concept came from influences rooted in Coco's modest background and early life experiences.

The work clothes that were worn by the adults around her helped convince Coco that all women, whatever their situation, needed less elaborate, more loosely fitting clothes for their increasingly active lives. "Women," Coco believed "were straight-jacketed by their clothes which made it impossible for them to move freely and forced them into dependence on their servants and their menfolk."

Her orphanage years instilled in her basic principles of well-made, modest clothes with uncluttered lines – a black hat, crisp white blouses with neat black ties at the neck, and simply styled jackets in plain fabrics. Coco believed in a degree of modesty, and although her early designs were daringly modern for the time, they were never brash or sexy.

Living the high life

After leaving the orphanage, Coco enjoyed the busy social life of her local town. After working hours, the vivacious young Coco sang popular songs in a café frequented by high-spirited, competitive, young officers looking for adventure. She enjoyed her popularity and even briefly held ambitions of making a career as a singer on the stage. Like most of the girls growing up in a garrison town at the turn of the century, Coco was impressed by

Fine horses and cavalry officers fascinated and attracted young Coco Chanel. She was influenced by the style of dress, impressed by the military tunics with their ornate braiding and flattering cut. Coco brought such details into her own designs, extending the barriers of fashion.

good-looking swaggering officers, especially cavalry officers in their dashing uniforms. She admired their gold-buttoned, braided tunics, well-tailored breeches, and high, polished boots.

The glamorous military tunics made a deep impression and undoubtedly became the inspiration behind Coco's famous braided suits of later decades.

Early influences

The cavalry, fine horses, and daring riders fascinated and attracted Coco Chanel. She learned to ride well and soon had several boyfriends in the cavalry world.

Coco quickly moved up the social ladder. When she was in her twenties, Coco started an important relationship with a rich, good-looking Englishman, Boy Capel. Boy was well known as a polo player and part of the affluent equestrian set.

Coco liked the easy, functional elegance of Boy's riding clothes – his soft and unstructured shirts, cashmere sweaters, comfortable jodhpurs, breeches, and well-crafted riding boots. She adopted a boyish style for herself, wearing open-necked men's shirts and riding astride in breeches at a time when women only rode sidesaddle in flowing riding habits. She also had Boy's riding jackets copied for herself. They suited her so well she decided to have them made in a variety of fabrics for general wear.

Young designer

By 1910, Coco Chanel's very individual style of sports jackets, open-necked shirts, skirts short enough to clear the ground, mannish raincoats, and simple, but eye-catching hats had been noticed by young fashion-conscious women in Paris and the exclusive French resorts. Her hats were less elaborate than the usual fashion of the time. They relied far more on shape, shade, and fabric.

Coco was so fresh and appealing in her youthful outfits that she tended to make other women look too fussy and overdressed. Interest in trying her new unconventional style was growing.

Coco's ambition to shine in her own right was greatly encouraged and she started to design, make, and sell hats in a small way from her own apartment. To please her and help her become more established, one of her boyfriends and Boy Capel set her up in her first professional business venture as a hat designer in the rue Cambon in Paris in 1910. This street was to be associated with her name for over fifty years. She soon had a growing clientele of smart young women. Coco herself appeared in the October 1910 issue of *Comoedia Illustre* showing her hats. Some of Coco's hats were worn in stage productions, and other French fashion magazines started to feature her designs.

A portrait of Coco Chanel. It was said that she acquired her nickname from the brief period she spent on stage. The unusual name suited the attractive, avant-garde designer, who was fast making her mark on the world.

One of Chanel's early hat designs in 1912 displayed by actress Gabrielle Dorziat. Coco Chanel wanted to earn herself a living rather than be supported by a man. She was already showing her creative flair, designing many hats for her women friends. Dorziat agreed to help bring Chanel's designs to the public by wearing them on stage, providing Chanel with an invaluable source of advertising.

The business in the rue Cambon soon expanded to incorporate clothes as well as hats. Coco worked as a couturier which meant that she designed individual items – skirts, dresses, hats – as once only designs. Her designs were not turned into hundreds of items and sold into boutiques. They were original, single purchases for the wealthy women of high society. This kind of fashion is also known as *haute couture,* or high fashion. Coco had to employ three seamstresses to work on fittings with her. She never designed from sketches – she always worked with the material on the model.

Coco soon had to recruit the services of her sister, Antoinette. When not in the work room, Antoinette would wear Coco's latest creations to the most fashionable parts of town so that women would notice her. It worked as an early form of advertising, and Coco Chanel found her business succeeding.

Expansion

In 1913, with the financial help of Boy Capel, thirty year old Coco Chanel opened a boutique selling her hats and her sportswear designs in the seaside resort of Deauville. She chose the most fashionable street, rue Gontaut Biron, where all the top hotels and casinos were located. She put up a white awning for shade from the sun; on it her name was spelled out in simple black letters. This was the beginning of the Chanel logo.

Chanel thoroughly enjoyed her design and business life, but the outside world saw it as the creative "interest" of Boy Capel's girlfriend rather than the beginning of a serious business career. The outbreak of World War I in 1914 soon helped to change this attitude.

In the later months of 1914, society women and their families, who were hoping to avoid the war zones in the rest of France, took refuge in Deauville. Life in the resort town on the English Channel changed dramatically. Many hotels were turned into hospitals for the war wounded. Women of all classes took up nursing and war work, and the fashions of the previous season were frivolous and cumbersome for practical work.

Chanel quickly saw the need for more suitable clothes and she opened up a workroom to produce a few basic designs – pullover tops, cardigans, and sailor-type jackets. These were all styles that she had been wearing for some time and they were all based on men's clothes. These practical designs suited the times and women's more active wartime lives; they were an instant success. Demand exceeded supply, and Chanel was soon planning a further extension of her growing fashion business.

As members of high society sought refuge from the war in towns such as Deauville, Coco Chanel found that she had the perfect opportunity to promote her more relaxed and casual fashions.

Coco Chanel and Boy Capel in 1912. In both her lifestyle and own fashion, Coco was led by what felt comfortable and natural. She was a keen horsewoman and thought it only sensible to sit astride the horse, as opposed to side-saddle. For this purpose, she took to wearing breeches, quite revolutionary for a woman at this time. Her quirky, impetuous character would not only enable her to stand out in how she conducted herself, but also in how she conducted her business.

Empire building

In the summer of 1915, Boy was given leave from the army and took Coco to Biarritz for a break.

The elegant resort town near the French-Spanish border, far away from the fighting, was crowded and bustling. It was filled with refugees, newly rich war profiteers, soldiers on leave, and prosperous Spanish visitors.

There was a feeling of escapism, of wanting to live for the day and have a good time. Shops, cafés, and bars were hectically busy, and the daring tango was danced every night in the big hotels.

Boy and Coco decided it was the ideal place to open the third Chanel fashion business and it was to be the most ambitious so far. Rather than opening another boutique like the one in Deauville, Chanel decided to open a couture house. It was lavishly set in an impressive villa near the casino. It had two workrooms, each with about thirty staff from the premier to the apprentices. Each dress sold for approximately three thousand francs.

It was an expensive project and Coco, now thirty-two, was determined to make a success of it and show Boy what a good investment he had made. She threw herself into her work with great energy and enthusiasm. She persuaded her sister, Antoinette, to help run the new business. They did a considerable amount of commuting between Paris and Biarritz to ensure the high quality of the new Chanel staff. Apart from Coco's frequent organizing trips to overview the two fashion houses, expert cutters, fitters, and tailors were sent from Paris to teach the new team. The local trainee seamstresses also went to the Paris workrooms to improve and refine their dressmaking skills.

Perfect timing

Fabrics and trimmings that were no longer available in wartime France were bought from nearby neutral Spain. These added a sense of seduction to the first collection, which was launched in September 1915.

Despite the high prices, it was an immediate

money-making success. French and Spanish women, including members of the Spanish court, eagerly flocked to buy Chanel's pretty, youthful-looking designs. They were unique. There was a great shortage of desirable clothes so there was no real competition. Coco's timing was perfect.

Biarritz and all the Chanel businesses thrived. By the end of 1916 there were over three hundred employees. Coco, much to Boy's surprise, repaid her loans, and with great satisfaction she became a financially independent businesswoman.

She was becoming well known as a radically inventive young designer. Her great skills were with materials, and she was the first to adapt underwear as outer garments. She styled jersey material, which until then had only been made into

Comfortable to wear and stylish to look at, Chanel's designs of 1916 were a commercial success. The theme of open-necked shirts, unstructured jersey jackets and skirts was one that could be adapted in a number of ways to suit different people.

With so many men called to join the armed services, women looked after the "Home Front," many working for the first time in barbershops, restaurants, and factories. As women's roles changed, World War I fashions became more practical. Chanel was able to build on this, providing clothes that were radical in their simplicity.

men's underwear, into her high-fashion suits and dresses. The demand for her jersey pieces became so great that she opened two jersey factories, one named Tricots Chanel and the other Tissus Chanel. Jersey was an affordable fabric which meant that Coco's designs were easily copied by the ready-to-wear market and could be bought by almost anyone. By this time, she also used a synthetic material named rayon in her work. Again this made the designs less expensive and allowed the Chanel style to be copied in all walks of life.

When designing, Coco was always conscious of the importance of practical clothes. She took the simple underslip chemise shape for her loose-waisted, easy fitting, calf-length day dresses. In 1917, as air raids became more frequent and intense, she introduced casual suits for women to wear in air raid shelters. It was the start of a new and different fashion for women that Chanel helped to make increasingly popular in the 1920s and 1930s.

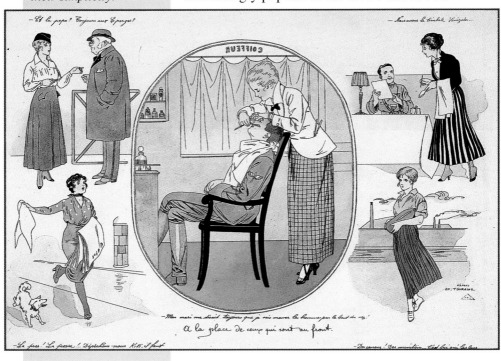

Public image and private sorrow

Coco Chanel had emerged as a successful designer and well known personality. She was very individual, confidently forging ahead with her career, always stunningly presented with newly bobbed hair and simple, chic clothes – the perfect advertisement for her designs.

Her private life was far less happy. In 1918, after over eight years with Coco, Boy Capel decided to marry someone else, an English society woman named Diana Wyndham. Coco appeared to accept the situation and continued to see Boy. The following year she received an even more devastating blow – just before Christmas 1919, Boy was killed in a car crash in the south of France.

Coco's grief was unbearable. She visited the site of the crash and cried for many hours. Later she had her bedroom entirely decorated in black as a sign of mourning. Her grief and terrible sense of loss were emotions she shared with many women at this time. Fathers, brothers, husbands, and sons had been killed in the war. In some families all the male members were wiped out, and countless women were left to fend for themselves in the postwar world.

Fame and recognition

A hardened and even more ambitious and determined Coco Chanel faced the 1920s. It proved to be one of the most exciting and fulfilling decades of her life.

In her impressive couture houses she now employed the kind of society women who would have looked down on her ten years earlier because of her humble beginnings. As her business as a designer developed, so did her confidence. Her style was unquestionably a major influence for fashion-conscious women. The stately, well-covered, elaborately dressed mature woman who had been the fashion ideal for so long was now considered an old-fashioned, out-of-touch image of the previous generation. The new ideal, popularized by Chanel herself, was slim, elegant, and youthful, with short

Coco Chanel's 1919 design already has a twenties look. She imposed her own style, influencing trends by the clothes she made and wore herself.

neat hair and a much more obvious use of makeup, particularly bright red lipstick.

Chanel established a range of classic twentieth century basic styles – flatteringly cut tailored jackets, easy fitting overblouses, knitted tops, practical length wraparound or pleated skirts, and slip-like sheath dresses. All Chanel's details were important and useful; the cuffs, buttons and pockets were where the wearer expected to find them. Coco was designing in large numbers and working hard. "Chanel works with ten fingers, with her nails, with her palms, pins and scissors, right on the dress. . . . Sometimes she falls to her knees in front of her work and grasps it firmly, not to worship it, but to punish it a little more," remembered her friend Colette.

Not everyone approved of the new concept or the expense of such unpretentious clothes. Paul Poiret, famed for his flamboyant styles of the early 1900s, called the Chanel look *"la pauvreté de luxe,"* or poverty deluxe. Coco herself declared her recipe for elegance and chic to be a blend of "austerity and natural purity" with natural tones – "beige in skintones," "pinks of roses," "blues from the sky," and "red blood tones."

The Russian influence

Despite Chanel's creative authority and business sense, she still found herself and her designs influenced by the man in her life. During the early 1920s she was romantically involved with the Grand Duke Dimitri Pavlovich.

He could have come straight out of a lavish Hollywood epic; a tall handsome twenty-nine year old aristocrat and a relation of the late Czar of Russia, he had been brought up in the Russian Court. He had also been personally chosen by the Czar as one of the elite guards officers. Pavlovich had fled from Russia just before the Revolution in 1917.

Although he had lost everything, and the contrast between their early lives could not have been greater, Coco was enthralled by Dimitri. His background inspired her "Slavic" period, which featured fur trimmings, Russian-style shirts and overblouses,

The Grand Duke Dimitri Pavlovich, with his movie star good looks, was the man in Chanel's life in the early 1920s. Chanel let her personal life and the people around her influence her creative designs, yet she rarely let her personal relationships get in the way of her independence and devotion to her work.

Coco Chanel (left) with her friend, Lady Abdy. Chanel started the idea of dressing up simple everyday clothes with designer, fake accessories.

embroidered tunics, and Russian jewel designs. Coco started a style for wearing fake pearl necklaces, a number at a time, along with ornate, fake jewel brooches, pins, and bracelets. These accessories, made to look like real stones and gems in ornate settings, are known as costume jewels. In 1924, Coco opened up a workshop to manufacture her costume accessories. She was the first to bring this area of fashion into the couture business and make it a profitable part of the fashion industry.

New directions

With her reputation as one of the most directional designers of the 1920s firmly established, Chanel began to look for ways of enhancing and building on her business. Unusually for a designer, she managed to combine an artistic temperament with a sharp business sense. Her diversification into the perfume industry proved to be the most important business undertaking of her life. In 1924, the Chanel perfume

"She couldn't draw or make sketches, but she could tell what was right and what was wrong with one glance ... she immediately knew what needed to be changed, what had to be worked on. Her talent was in her hands and in her eyes."

Axel Madsen, from Coco Chanel – A Biography.

Coco loved the smart resort life. In her usual manner, she managed to convince everyone else that they loved it too. Her designer outfits and beachwear started a whole new fashion category.

company began a long relationship with the largest perfume factory in France, owned by Pierre Wertheimer, as Parfums Chanel. Her fortune was to be built on her creation, Chanel No. 5.

Before No. 5, perfume was based on floral scents. Women would smell of one flower or a combination of several. Although the products were highly concentrated, they faded quickly. So people tended to be overscented on arrival at social functions.

Chanel believed her perfume should be an expression of her fashion concept and complement the spirit of contemporary art and design. "A woman who doesn't wear perfume has no future" was one of Coco's many sayings.

Her fragrance was created from natural animal and plant essences combined with many synthetic products. Over eighty ingredients made up the new formula, making it possible to use smaller, less overpowering amounts. It was an exciting new invention for a very modern designer – just what Coco had hoped for. The all-important design of the bottle was also suitably advanced. Scent had always been put into ornate shapes. The simple, unadorned cube, and the clean-cut, eye-catching graphics on the label made the Chanel bottle a classic design that still looked modern seventy years after it was launched.

Coco considered five to be her lucky number – she always presented her collections of new designs on

Chanel's designs made a feature of simplicity. These collarless 1925 outfits (above left) are a clear example of Chanel's minimalist style, while the 1920s outfit (above right) highlights the Russian influence with the coronet style hat and a fur trimmed cape.

February 5 and August 5. This theory worked again with Chanel No. 5 as it became the perfume of the decade. By 1929 it had become the best selling perfume in the world and remained one of the most famous and commercially successful of the century.

The Duke of Westminster

Now in her forties, Chanel had become a part of the rich and famous international set. The Prince of Wales and Sir Winston Churchill were among her many illustrious friends. Her income was large enough for her to support several members of her family and have beautiful homes including a stunning built-to-order villa called *La Pausa* in the exclusively smart French Riviera. She loved the fashionable resort life and personally popularized the deep suntan and designer beachwear.

In Monte Carlo in 1925, she was introduced by mutual friends to the Duke of Westminster. He was reputed to be "the richest man in England" and lived in considerable style. When they met he had just divorced his second wife. He was intrigued by Coco Chanel: her chic, quick wit and her life as a famous designer and powerful independent businesswoman fascinated him.

English influences

Coco was also impressed by the Duke and flattered by his obvious attraction to her. Once again, her relationship influenced her designing and she decided to make the "English" style into an important fashion statement – country-looking, casual jackets, simple matching sweaters and skirts, specially commissioned British checks and tweeds, were all interpreted into the soft, flattering Chanel concept, variations of which have remained permanently in fashion.

Although the relationship between the Duke of Westminster and Coco Chanel was known to have its ups and downs, it was serious and important to both of them. Marriage was certainly a possibility, but Chanel was not prepared to give up her business

A clever 1920s caricature of Coco, drawn inside the outline of her well known Chanel No. 5 perfume bottle.

career and become dependent on a man. "God knows I wanted love. But the moment I had to choose between the man I loved and my dresses, I chose the dresses," Chanel revealed. "Work has always been a kind of a drug for me, even if I wonder what Chanel would have been without the men in my life." The Duke desperately wanted a male heir, which it was not possible for Coco to provide. After much heart-searching they decided to end their five-year romance.

Fashion changes

Although the 1920s had their share of instability and problems they are best remembered for their youthful optimism and innovation. But the Wall Street stock market crash of October 1929 triggered

"Chanel No. 5, to me, is still the ideal scent for a woman. She can wear it anywhere, anytime, and everybody . . . loves it. No one has gone beyond Chanel No. 5."
Diana Vreeland, editor, from the American Vogue.

Above: By the beginning of the 1930s, fashions were moving away from the basic, uncluttered designs. The onset of the Hollywood era with its dazzling designs also influenced fashions, as more ornate decorations were added to outfits.

Opposite: In 1937, at the age of fifty-four, Chanel was still creating sought-after designs, but her position as trend-setter was being challenged by up-and-coming designers.

the worldwide Depression of the 1930s, and a much more uncertain, troubled decade.

Fashion reflected the changing mood of the times with softer, more wistful, slightly older lines – draped necklines, a more body-conscious fit with normal waistlines, and longer, gently flared skirts. Chanel once again used her business instinct to make a bold statement. Despite the shortage of money and feeling of gloom, she introduced real jewels into her accessory range. But each piece, a brooch or clasp, could be converted into another accessory. In 1929 she opened a boutique in one of the rue Cambon couture buildings for these accessories, which also sold belts, quilted purses, and scarves.

The real thing

Having turned her attention to the real thing – diamonds – a private viewing was held complete with armed security guards. The designs were impressively luxurious. Bracelets looked like broad glittering cuffs, necklaces were designed to sit at the base of the neck and spread out over the shoulders like sparkling stars, and pendants were styled to look like a sunburst of white stones at the end of a long chain. Private customers and international dealers attended the show, and Chanel's inventive ideas inspired a new, very 1930s design.

Chanel creations of the early 1930s were admired worldwide as the ultimate sophisticated high-fashion look. Although she produced some of her most beautiful flattering styles, her design concept was becoming less revolutionary and more in the mainstream of the new decade's fashion trends.

Branching out

The 1930s were also the golden age of the cinema with its worldwide influence and idolized movie stars. In 1931, Chanel was asked to design clothes for American films by the well known, powerful producer, Samuel Goldwyn. She was eventually persuaded to go to Hollywood for a guaranteed contract of one million dollars.

Even though there were less expensive Hollywood film designers available, Goldwyn was prepared to pay Chanel such a huge fee because he wanted to offer the best fantasy world to movie audiences.

It was the height of the great Depression, millions were out of work, and the big studios had to compete for audiences. The public was offered escapist films to help them forget their troubles. A dream world was portrayed on the big screen showing extremely attractive, glamorous people with sex appeal and leading lives full of drama, fun, and romance.

Hollywood

Coco was the most celebrated designer of the age and Goldwyn believed having his most famous stars stunningly dressed by Chanel would give him a distinct publicity advantage over his rivals.

Despite the hype, the association was not as successful as had been hoped. The designs, although stylish, were criticized for being too underplayed; the movie moguls thought they weren't sufficiently rich and showy. The *New Yorker* magazine claimed, "Chanel, the famous Paris couturier, makes a lady look like a lady; Hollywood wants a lady to look like two ladies."

Although initially disappointing, both sides learned from the experience – Chanel understood the importance of making her designs a little bolder and more photogenic, and Hollywood learned the value of dressing its newer, sophisticated stars in slow-to-date, quieter, elegant clothes, which were to prove ideal for the more mature mood of many classic 1930s and 1940s movies.

Threat

As the decade progressed, Chanel's position as fashion leader and modern guru was seriously challenged by the Paris-based, lively Italian designer Elsa Schiaparelli, whose reputation had been growing for several years. By the mid 1930s her bolder style of bright clothes with very wide shoulders and frivolous themes – which included a

Chinese influence, mock military uniforms, and circus themes – made fashion headlines. It was a real alternative to Chanel's understatement. Much to Coco's annoyance, "Schap" was becoming the new darling of the ultra-chic and a threat to her authority.

Rivalry between the designers was intense. Every season there was speculation about whose collection was the best and the most trendsetting. Coco Chanel, always strong and determined, fought for her supremacy and rose to the occasion. In the late 1930s her creativity was at a new high. She produced some of her most brilliant and successful collections. She had adapted and updated her styles to the new romantic mood sweeping the fashion world. Her padded shoulders, puffed sleeves, nipped-in waists, peplummed velvet suits, and particularly her boned-bodice, full-skirted, neo-Victorian evening dresses were a far cry from the slim, boyish lines that had first made her famous twenty years earlier.

Suits, dresses, and coats – fashions for the young – displayed in the spring collection of 1933. These designs by Chanel's contemporary, Paul Poiret, reflect the influence of the freer styles encouraged by Chanel herself.

A mature romance

Chanel was already in her early fifties, but couldn't have been further removed from the conventional idea of the middle-aged woman. Although formidable and hard looking, she was slim, always faultlessly presented, immaculately groomed, and superbly dressed.

Secure in her own wealth and luxurious lifestyle, she seemed less impressed by aristocratic super-rich men, preferring the company of politicians, intellectuals, and artists.

The important man in her life at this time was Paul Iribarnegaray, better known by his pseudonym, "Iribe." He was an artist, satirical cartoonist, and art and design expert, and a match for Coco's wit and intellect. They were a well-suited couple and many people expected them to marry. Chanel was beginning to come around to the idea when fate once again dealt her private life a severe blow. Iribe, who was the same age as Coco, died unexpectedly from a heart attack after playing an energetic game of tennis. For the third time, circumstances beyond her control had deprived Coco of the committed relationship of marriage.

The strike

The mid and late 1930s were politically troubled times for France. The problem of unemployment and the effects of the Depression dragged on and extremist communist and fascist agitators added to the atmosphere of instability.

Strikes affected industry, the public services and eventually textiles and retailing. A left-wing government was elected and workers pressed for improved working conditions, higher wages, and recognition of their unions.

Chanel was unsympathetic to the situation of the workers. Although she had come from underprivileged beginnings herself, she felt she had worked hard for her success and had never been given anything through politically orchestrated workers' rights. By 1938 she had four thousand

Coco Chanel, drawn by the English illustrator, fashion photographer, and designer Cecil Beaton. Highlighting all the Chanel style features, he also included her ever-ready pair of scissors!

29

German occupying troops sit among the locals on the Paris metro in the early 1940s. Away from the front, life seemed to go on almost as normal – designs were still going in and out of fashion, but Coco Chanel was temporarily not involved. At the start of World War II, and for the next fifteen years, Chanel did not present any new collections.

employees and was selling in Europe, the United States, South America, and the Middle East.

When fifty of her workers went on strike, she refused all their demands and took refuge in the Ritz Hotel. A delegation presented itself at the hotel, but she would not see any of them. They were told that Mademoiselle Chanel would meet them at the couture house when she was ready. Dressed with great care, and defiantly wearing one of her "Number one" suits rather than her usual work "Number two" suits, she confronted the strikers outside the fashion house, to which she was denied access by a picket line.

Coco was furious at being shut out of her own business. Despite having come from a similar background to many of her staff, she had no sympathy for them. The workers requested a weekly salary, paid time off, limited working hours, and contracts of employment. In response to these

requests, Coco fired three hundred of them. Reluctantly, however, and faced with missing a collection, Coco Chanel had to give in to some of her workers' demands for new employment conditions. It was the only way she could ensure her next collection would be presented on time.

Pride as well as money was at stake, and she could not risk allowing Schiaparelli, her arch rival who was having far fewer problems with her smaller staff, to grab the stage of Paris fashion and become the unchallenged designer of the season.

War and occupation

The outbreak of World War II, in September 1939, did not produce the immediate fierce fighting of 1914 or the devastating bombing of French cities. It was not until the following spring that the real shooting war got under way.

Above: Victorious German troops marching down the Champs Élysées, Paris, in 1940.

*Above and opposite top:
Chanel's Paris apartment
over her salon in the
rue Cambon was
expensively furnished
with impressive antiques,
sculptures, and highly
decorated ornaments.*

In the meantime, life in Paris assumed a subdued normality and the Paris fashion houses presented their collections as usual. It was to be Chanel's last for fifteen years. In 1939, she declared it to be "no time for fashion" although she had founded her success during World War I.

France was occupied by the German army from 1940–1944, but society life, plays, nightclubs, and fashionable race meetings all continued. Couture houses stayed open and despite restrictions and shortages they produced chic, desirable clothes. Many designers prospered and Chanel could surely have done the same. Nazi officers eagerly bought bottles of Chanel No. 5 for their girlfriends and wives. Chanel was not anti-German. It was just before the war had started that she had begun a long-term relationship with Hans Gunther von Dincklage, an influential German stationed in Paris. Von D. was a cultivated, attractive man, tall and blond with a Hanoverian father and an English

Left: Paris's world famous Ritz Hotel featured many times in Chanel's life. She made the hotel her home from 1930 until she died in 1971.

mother, and a reputation as a charming womanizer. He had spent a lot of time in France and was fluent in French and English. He worked for Hitler's government before and during the war, and although it was never proved, he was believed to have been a spy and was certainly considered useful enough to be kept in Paris throughout the occupation.

Although von D. was thirteen years younger than Coco there was a strong mutual attraction. They seemed content with one another's company and lived comfortably at the Ritz Hotel, which was reserved mainly for occupation officials.

This sobering notice announces in both German and French that anyone suspected of Resistance activity will be shot. This message highlighted the reality of the war, which, to some still living the high life, could occasionally be too easily forgotten.

Takeover attempt

During the occupation, Chanel was reputed to have tried to gain full control of her perfume company.

For fifteen years Pierre Wertheimer and his brother manufactured and sold Chanel perfumes. Although the Wertheimers had fled the German persecution of the Jewish people and were living in the United States, their interests were well looked after in wartime France, and the take-over failed.

This caused much bitterness in their long association with Coco Chanel. She was a cunning businesswoman with a fixed goal, "All or nothing." After several more years of wrangling, Chanel accepted a 2% royalty on the gross sales of her perfumes worldwide. With Chanel No. 5 being the best selling perfume in the world, Coco Chanel now in her sixties, became a woman with a colossal income from her perfumes alone, with no further need to work.

Still influencing

Fashion continued to evolve in the war years. In Paris, high hats, particularly large draped turbans were worn with flared or draped skirts. In Britain and the United States, with many women involved in war work, simple clean-cut easier lines predominated – rolled up hairstyles, male-looking tailored suits, and

A portrait of a happy, relaxed, and older Chanel, timelessly dressed in her neat white-cuffed suit.

uncluttered dresses livened up off-duty occasions with small tilted hats and costume necklaces and brooches. Hemlines were shortened to just below the kneecap and style returned to the practical Chanel concept of the mid-1920s.

After the war, Chanel and her boyfriend took refuge in neutral Switzerland to avoid investigation and possible persecution for her associations with the Germans. In France, there was understandably a highly charged emotional need for punishing anyone suspected to have been a collaborator. Fearing that it would be thought they fell into this category, the couple chose to remain in Switzerland.

Her difficulties in France, however, did not seem to have much effect on her international reputation as a fashion icon, and Coco must have been delighted to have her exile in Switzerland cheered up by reports from Paris on the booming sales of Chanel No. 5. American and British troops snapped up every available bottle in liberated France just as the conquering Germans had done four years before. Chanel No. 5 was such a well known name and perhaps even more important, easier to ask for by non-French speaking troops.

Picking up the pieces

The position of European fashion and, in particular, Paris's traditional leadership was open to question after 1945 and the end of the war.

Many cities lay devastated. Europe was poor and it seemed unlikely that it would ever be able to support the luxurious "high society" way of life that couture fashion depended on. The powerful and affluent United States was now the most important market for expensive stylish clothes. New York was the place for high fashion and Hollywood was full of movie star beauty.

The most valued clients in the fashion world had become American manufacturers and store buyers rather than individual customers. Buyers usually took twice-yearly trips to the couture collections of Paris. Designs were for the American market and Paris models soon became a feature in quality stores throughout the United States. Copies and ideas from Paris designers were also a major influence on the entire women's clothing industry.

New materials were also available. Before the war, silk, wool, and cotton were the main fabrics in use; after the war, synthetic materials that were waterproof, drip-dry, nylon, or permanently pleated were new tools to work with. Coco "wanted to be at the front of the revolution."

"When I think of work, I think of the women I try to dress, not the couture house. . . . Once I helped liberate women, I'll do it again."

Coco Chanel.

The New Look

In 1947, Christian Dior, backed and promoted by one of France's largest textile manufacturers, created his legendary "New Look." Breasts were pushed out, waists pulled tightly in, and immensely full skirts flared out to near ankle length. Confining figure-shaping underwear – uplift bras, corselettes, and several petticoats – were needed to achieve the shape. Much to Coco's dismay, fashion was returning to a pre-Chanel concept.

It must have been strange for Chanel, the great innovator, to be so completely out of fashion. She thought the New Look was absurd and the idea of putting women back into corsets a backward step, totally unsuited to the modern world.

Christian Dior's "New Look" of 1947 exaggerated curves – the long, full skirts returning fashion temporarily to the pre-Chanel concept.

37

The manufacturing process of a perfume can be long and difficult. Coco Chanel was influential in the development of her own perfume, Chanel No. 5. She and the owner of a laboratory, Ernest Beaux, experimented with a number of artificial fragrances. This revolutionized the perfume-making process, which usually relied on the costly and time-consuming process of extracting scent from real flowers.

Most people loved the New Look. It was a natural reaction to the years of uniforms and austerity. Women thoroughly enjoyed wearing their small-waisted fluted jackets and long, swirling skirts. Chanel-type fashions of the 1920s – once thought so modern and progressive – were now ridiculed. The famous fashion photographer, stage designer, and style critic, Cecil Beaton, summed up the attitude: "Never have the fashions of a previous era been so loudly condemned and thought so downright ugly."

Exile

Coco was very secure financially. As well as her current income from perfume sales, past earnings for the foreign sales of her perfume Chanel No. 5 during World War II had accumulated substantially in her Swiss bank accounts. She was richer than ever and could afford to live anywhere and buy anything she wanted, but she was "bored to death."

Although financial security had always been very important to her, these years were not happy ones for Coco. Her inactive life as an exile in Switzerland did not suit her temperament. She looked noticeably older and less stunningly presented. She missed her work and the stimulation of the Paris fashion world and her position as a celebrated international figure.

Some of her closest, long-standing friends died at this time. They had been very much a part of her life during her glamorous triumphant years and their departure seemed to be yet another indication that her period of fame and achievement was finished and already part of the history of another era.

Chanel rediscovered

By 1950 the romantic charm of the New Look had waned. Fashion continued to be based on figure-accentuating lines, but the need for clothes designed to suit the age once again influenced the developing fashion trends.

The 1920s were looked at with new interest; the young generation growing up after the war saw them as amusing and wacky, rather than ugly and

unflattering. Designers sensing the changing mood began to show a fun influence from the Roaring Twenties. *Vogue* noted the change of direction: "Hair is short, the cigarette holder long and the first Chanel over-shirts ... have been seen in the resorts."

Fashion and the changing times were once again moving Chanel's way and beginning to rediscover her unique concept.

Coco Chanel became less of a reclusive exile. She visited the United States and spent more time in France, particularly at her villa on the Riviera.

Why did she decide at the age of seventy to reopen her couture house and become a seriously

committed designer again? The reason for her return, she declared, was to give back to women the freedom of easy-fitting clothes. Fashion was already moving this way, but declining interest in her perfume as fame faded may well have been the most compelling reason. In addition, she was still vital, energetic, and missed her status as a famous personality and directional designer.

Chanel showed her much publicized return collection on February 5, 1954.

Outdated?

The collection was not well received. Many people felt it was a mistake and thought Coco should have left the Chanel legend of earlier decades intact.

Some of the fashion press were brutally frank – they thought her designing was out of touch, from another period, even old-ladyish. Typically unflattering comments included statements such as "melancholy retrospective," "a fiasco," and "out in the sticks with Chanel."

A less determined person would have been devastated by such harsh criticism. Coco had great inner strength, she was level-headed, and had always fought for success and recognition. Her reaction to the bad press was to start immediately on her next collection. In her practical and unassuming way, she found consolation in hard work. During the following two seasons she got back into her stride as a designer and adapted her concept of understatement and relaxed fit to the fashion mood of the 1950s.

Knowing the market

The American market, which already catered for independent, trendsetting women, soon welcomed the easy-to-wear, flattering elegance of Chanel's revamped styles. "At seventy-one Gabrielle Chanel is creating more than a fashion: a revolution," praised the U.S. magazine, *Life*. The distinctive Chanel suit was particularly popular – day versions made from specially woven fabrics were often trimmed with glittering, military-style gold, and silver braiding edged the glamorous brocade evening outfits.

Chanel's evening suits such as these were equally admired. They had fresh appeal to women who were used to rigid tailoring, and Chanel's beautifully made couture designs became great fashion status symbols. The designs and styles were often worn by international society women, models, and movie stars.

During Chanel's non-designing years there had been a considerable amount of restructuring and development in the fashion world. The Paris couturiers had regained the creative lead and still dressed individual clients. Their most commercially valuable role, however, was as a super design source for wholesale manufacturers. The clothing industry

Above: Chanel was a perfectionist and spent much time selecting and developing fabrics for her designs.

Opposite: After a shaky relaunch in 1954, Chanel's styles, like these from the late fifties, received international acclaim. Her designs became a growing influence in wholesale manufacturing worldwide.

was expanding rapidly and developing into one of the world's most important trades.

Manufacturers commercialized the fashion trends with mass marketing. Realizing the potential of haut couture designs, they made direct copies and simplified versions for all price ranges. These couture based designs gradually became best selling ready-to-wear suits, popular in Europe and the United States.

Chanel was not daunted by this growing trend in the fashion world. By the end of the decade she had re-established herself as a newsworthy designer and, for the second time in her life, was about to become a major influence on fashion. This was highlighted in 1957 when Chanel was awarded the Neiman Marcus award for the designer who had made the greatest contribution to twentieth century fashion.

Street fashion

Chanel had been the first designer to adapt so-called "street fashion" – work-wear, traditional men's styles, country clothes, and sports garments had all inspired her more practical approach to designing clothes for everyday life. The 1960s was the most revolutionary decade since the 1920s, and for the first time fashion changes went beyond Chanel's refined concept.

Beatnik, baby-doll, space-age, and hippie styles appealed to a more liberated, rebellious generation. Streetwise beatnik and biker gear, such as black leather, black sweaters, denim, and boots, inspired young designers like Mary Quant and Yves St. Laurent.

The baby-doll woman had bouffant hair, false eyelashes, and flimsy mini-length printed smock dresses that finished just above the knees.

"Space age" designs were popular in the late 1960s. Designers such as the Frenchman André Courrèges and Spain's Paco Rabanne, pushed forward the frontiers of fashion. Having established themselves in the fashion world, it was then easier for them to experiment and still be taken seriously. Rabanne was particularly interested in creating clothes using modern materials such as this plastic disc dress.

Chanel's 1964 designs show her subtle use of tones and cleverly coordinated fabrics.

The hippie generation took its ethnic looks from traditional African and Asian styling – permed hair, flowing caftans, beads, rings, bells, and garlands of love and peace flowers.

Chanel left the pop-age design well alone and concentrated on making her own distinctive style even more attractive.

She offered women a welcome alternative. Her clothes suited all age groups and were especially flattering and youthful to older women who felt ignored by many 1960s fashion trends.

Perfectionist

Chanel's designs were less austere looking than those of other leading couturiers. She survived the miniskirt by saying the length of the skirt should always depend on the length of the leg. She used subtle wools and tweeds, lightly interlined and attractively edged with contrasting wool or silk braiding. Jackets were often worn open; some of them were cut edge-to-edge without buttoned fastenings, but held together with a brooch-shaped clip. Suits were matched or toned with silky blouses with scarf collars or neckbands that tied into floppy bows. Skirts were cut with easy straightish lines, and had pockets in the front panels or side-seams. Hemlines covered the kneecaps – Coco thought bare knees ugly and unfeminine!

Coco was a perfectionist and the importance she placed on finding a fabric that pleased her sometimes went as far as cutting up a specially woven check, rearranging the pattern herself and then having it sewn together as an exclusive, unique design. She was also known to reposition the stripes and patterns of her distinctive braiding in the same way.

To complete the total look, Chanel purses in quilted leather with chain handles were carried, and slingback shoes with black leather or silk toecaps and beige suede uppers were worn. Hair was cut and sometimes tied back with a neat, black silk ribbon. Her style had great appeal. It did something for the wearers. It made them look more attractive and feel more confident about their appearance.

Chanel was one of the most copied designers of the period. She did not seem to mind the ever growing numbers of mass-produced Chanel-style suits and accessories. She was surprised and intrigued that she could exert so much influence at her age on such a youth-orientated era.

She knew copies would always be inferior to her original creations. A friend and customer introduced Coco to her daughter who was wearing a ready-made, medium-priced, Chanel copy. Coco looked it over with interest and declared it "Not bad," apart from the hang of the sleeves. She took the jacket and

Coco Chanel's life story was staged in a Broadway show in 1969. Here, a model stands on the staircase in the show, a replica of the famous staircase where the new collections were often presented.

proceeded to personally reset the sleeves to her satisfaction. They were then resewn into the jacket by one of Chanel's expert seamstresses and the corrected garment was handed back to her friend's delighted daughter.

The ultimate style guru

By her seventies, Coco Chanel had become a legend in her own lifetime. She was revered as the ultimate style guru, having influenced the fashion trends for many years. She was also well known for her philosophical pronouncements, among which were, "You can be gorgeous at twenty, charming at forty, and irresistible for the rest of your life," and "In old age elegance and fastidiousness are a form of dignity. A young woman shouldn't be too elaborate – it's so dowdy."

Chanel's style, which was clearly based on and evolved from the designs she created in the 1920s and 1930s, now added to her authority. Fashions from earlier decades were constantly revived and were often credited as "Chanel-style" or "Chanel inspired."

Chanel in later life. She believed that life should be led to the full and often said, "After fifty you have to deserve your face."

Coco received many accolades for her work and was given several awards for her unique contribution to twentieth century fashion, some of which, much to the embarrassment of the publicity-seeking presenters, she turned down. She had refused the Fashion Immortal award in 1963 because it had been given to other designers.

The couture house was busy. Coco worked hard and long hours. "Sometimes I am so tired that when I fall asleep it is like falling down a well," she remembered. Clients were expected to order a minimum of two outfits per season. Many famous women were dressed by Chanel, including Jackie Kennedy. Mrs. Kennedy chose an attractive pink and navy outfit for her tour of Texas in November 1963, unaware that this would be tragically recorded for the history books due to the assassination of her husband, President John F. Kennedy.

> *"If fashion has taken a turn to the woman, no one can deny that much of the impetus for that turn stems from Coco Chanel – the fierce, wise, wonderful, and completely self-believing Chanel."*
> From Vogue, March 1959.

The final years

Producing her collections with dedicated staff in the reassuring atmosphere of her fashion house was everything to Coco in her later years. She found a sense of security in perfecting her craft and the Chanel image.

She carefully selected stunning girls to enhance her designs. Some of her models became friends, and hearing about their admirers and glamorous social lives delighted Coco. It was a way of reliving her own youthful experiences.

Although Coco loved her work as a couturier, she did not seem to have the interest or energy to take advantage of the opportunity to commercialize and sell the right to use her name for the hugely profitable mass market. This would be done with great success by others after her death.

Coco was thought to have been lonely in her last years. Many of her friends had died and her adventurous private life was all in the past. She lived quietly and always slept in a simple attic bedroom in the Ritz Hotel near her salon and private apartment. She was suffering with arthritis and took numerous vitamin pills every day. Coco Chanel had been working on her spring designs the day before she died on January 10, 1971, aged eighty-seven.

Coco Chanel had a successful and eventful life. She was one of the most remarkable businesswomen of the twentieth century. Lasting happiness in her private life, however, eluded her. Because of her deprived childhood, she may have feared deep personal commitment and was often quoted as saying, "I never looked so much for someone to love, as for somebody to love me."

End of an era

The "Swinging Sixties" fashions were followed in the early 1970s by brash "glam-rock" pop-star styles. Bright satin jackets decorated with diamanté clips, skintight velvet hotpants, widely flared jeans and exaggerated, triple-layered platform shoes and boots were all the height of young fashion when Coco died in 1971. They could not have been further from her concept of refined understatement.

Chanel's death marked the end of an era in twentieth century fashion. Her couture house – which still catered exclusively for individual customers who were willing to pay highly for intricately made, expertly fitted, personalized clothes – had been declining for some years. The timeless charm of Coco Chanel's designs and the charisma of her forceful personality had kept her couture business above the clashes of changing times and the commercialization of fashion.

During the 1960s most of the leading Paris designers had become involved in the ready-to-wear market. As well as extensive women's ranges, they also diversified into high quality men's and children's clothes, as well as accessories, lingerie, cosmetics, and items for the home. In 1978, Chanel moved into ready-to-wear.

With the decreasing number of private customers, the couture collections' real value was to catch attention at publicity presentations in order to show off the creative talents of commercialized designers. Their designer ready-to-wear ranges were now regarded as a more serious indication of the incoming fashion trends that would influence the all-important mass market.

Chanel after Coco

Yves St. Laurent was in the forefront of the modern business-structured fashion empires. He was a directional inventive designer and his Rive Gauche shops for men and women led the way in designer retailing. It was a pattern that the future Chanel shops followed. Under strict rules, St. Laurent shops opened in leading cities all over the world, and the licensees had to meet certain approved conditions at their own expense. The shops had to be rented in premier locations and arranged to exact specifications. They bought exclusively from each Rive Gauche collection and if their shops failed to generate an agreed annual turnover, the right to sell could be withdrawn and offered elsewhere.

Like many fashion people, Yves St. Laurent revered the Coco Chanel legend and her unique style. In homage to her and in recognition of her special contribution to fashion, he gave his 1972 collections a strong Chanel look.

During the next couple of years the 1970s recession set in, fashion calmed down and a more grown up mood prevailed. The Chanel Look had renewed appeal and began to influence many more European and American designers.

Cardigan-style jersey jackets, striped sweaters, soft blouses, gently flared below-the-knee length skirts, and tie-neck dresses with neat pleated skirts – all clearly inspired by Coco's designs of the 1920s and 1930s – once again became everyday basics in the mid-1970s.

The couture house

Although Chanel's influence in the fashion world was as strong as ever, her couture house lacked a sense of direction and purpose.

Several well-respected designers tried both to maintain and progress her image. It was an extremely difficult and unrewarding task. Their

"Chanel was completely in tune with the twentieth century, understanding the changes in the lifestyles of women and also understanding how her clothes should cater to them. Chanel had brought about a revolution in day wear."
Alice Mackrell, from Coco Chanel.

Above and opposite: The fashion trade is an extremely competitive industry to be in. Most aspiring designers attend fashion school, such as these in Italy (above) and China (opposite right). Here they receive professional training in the use of fabrics and how garments are made.

design brief was very limiting: to stay close to the spirit of Coco's last collections, but at the same time to offer the clientele enough innovations to keep them interested. If the designs were given a slightly more 1970s look, they were considered too far away from the Chanel image and if they stayed close to the established designs, they were criticized for being dull and static!

To add to this, many customers felt post-Coco Chanel designs inevitably lacked the magic of Coco's touch. It was a frustrating time for the house designers – a time when new fashion ideas were crucial for business.

"The designer's job is a difficult one. He has to satisfy two different groups. The press demands something new and forward-looking which will photograph well and look as different as possible from last year's look. The buyers also demand something new, but they want something as near as possible in spirit to the successful lines of last season."

Colin McDowell,
from McDowell's Directory of Twentieth Century Fashion.

German designer Karl Lagerfeld was appointed design director of the House of Chanel in 1983. He confidently imposed his style on Chanel merchandise for both the ready-to-wear and couture lines.

Needing a boost

During the 1980s, fashion became international and intensely competitive – more than eleven million people were employed in the fashion world. Paris held the lead for style, Milan was a close second with exciting new designers such as Giorgio Armani and Gianni Versace, New York's influence was gaining strength, and London was producing a new generation of important designers. Clothes were manufactured, imported, and exported all over the world and professional promotion, marketing, and retailing were essential. There was an ever increasing demand for designer merchandise and the value of brand names was more important than ever before.

Chanel's world famous name and Coco's well known influence on the century's fashions were unquestionably respected, but some said the Chanel clothes of the early 1980s failed to live up to their illustrious name. Many people at the time thought that their appeal had been fading for over ten years, the designs lacked sparkle and innovation, and they were out of touch with fashion's more assertive mood.

New design talent

The owners of Chanel felt it was time to rethink the business policy and decided to make sweeping changes to relaunch the Chanel image into the high-flying, money making, top end of the international fashion market. To achieve their aims they needed the help and talents of a well known designer with enough confidence and strength of character to make the transformation an assured success. In 1983 the House of Chanel chose the German designer Karl Lagerfeld. A new dynamic era began for Chanel.

Lagerfeld was employed to design for both the couture and the ready-to-wear collections. His interpretation of up-market fashion suited the times. He reshaped and updated the Chanel image to the "power-dressed" idea. He made expensive clothes look expensive and his designs clearly displayed the wearers' wealth for all to see.

The original Chanel cut was radically overhauled. Structured jackets with square, heavily padded shoulders and precise body shaping were decorated with shiny gilt buttons and buckles showing the Chanel logo. These showier jackets were teamed with tighter fitting, shorter skirts and strongly stated accessories.

Coco's soft subtle tones were supplemented with more black, classic navy, and stark white, as well as scarlet, fuchsia, and bright blue. Lagerfeld's eye-catching bright jackets trimmed with black and worn with brief black skirts, were a big hit with the new, dressed-for-success, free-spending Chanel customers.

Widening the influence

Lagerfeld turned to another famous Coco classic: the little black dress.

His versions were aimed at the confident woman who was proud of her worked-out, firmed-up shape. Sexy black dresses were body-fitted with scooped-out necklines, widely belted waists, and hip-clinging skirts. They were accessorized with bold costume jewels, sheer or lace-patterned black tights, and high-heeled shoes.

Lagerfeld was bold with his new fashion ideas for the House of Chanel. He was in tune with the mood and tastes of his clientele. Attitudes had changed radically – wearing sexy clothes was popular and extravagant dressing had become a perfectly acceptable fashion option.

All aspects of Chanel merchandise were revised to follow the trend for rich-looking, extrovert fashions. Gold, silver, or encrusted embroideries were used on jackets, dresses, handbags, and shoes. Larger, more ornate costume accessories were designed – bigger earrings, wider bracelets, and multi-stranded necklaces – all gilded and generously decorated with semi-precious stones or fake pearls.

It was a great commercial success and by the end of the decade Chanel retail outlets had multiplied worldwide. By 1988, Chanel was one of five leading fashion houses meeting the demands for couture

Chanel's Paris fashion house in the rue Cambon in 1994. This was where the Chanel name was originally stamped in 1910. Even within the competitive world of fashion, Coco Chanel and Chanel managed to influence fashion for generations.

Above: Three famous fashion personalities, supermodel Claudia Schiffer, Karl Lagerfeld, and Yasmin le Bon. In Chanel's time, collections were displayed in her own fashion houses. Her models would descend a flight of stairs, resplendent in their new outfits, while Chanel looked on from above. In Lagerfeld's time, the supermodels walked the catwalk, like Claudia Schiffer (opposite), wearing a wedding dress from the Chanel Winter 1994 couture collection.

orders. When Lagerfeld was taken on there were nineteen Chanel boutiques around the world; by 1990 that number had increased to more than forty. There were branches in France, Italy, Spain, Germany, Austria, Belgium, and England. In the United States alone there were over forty boutiques. Ten were launched in Japan. Chanel also became established in Canada, Hong Kong, Taiwan, Korea, Singapore, and Australia.

Keeping the faith?

The pluses and minuses of what Karl Lagerfeld did with Chanel have been keenly debated for many years. He was keen to impose his interpretation, while still maintaining Coco Chanel's style.

Chanel's style had a long-term effect on the way generations of women from all sections of society dressed, and her designs reflected the changing tempo and influences of women's lives during the first half of the century.

Later, in the 1960s, when new, dynamic young designers introduced revolutionary changes, Coco had retained her position in the fashion world and continued to be admired for the charm of her feminine clothes. She was a socially aware, intuitive woman's designer and her styles were always created to flatter women and improve the individual wearer's overall appearance.

Karl Lagerfeld was eager to meet the challenge of providing women with the fashionable designs in the same way Chanel had done. While he developed the Chanel image in his own way, he was concerned that he should "create a better future with elements of the past." He was full of ideas, trends and fashion experiments. As Chanel had influenced the styles and designs of her time, Lagerfeld believed he was in tune with the desires of the modern world. He presented his look of the season for women to follow. While some of the styles may have surprised Coco Chanel herself, Lagerfeld's high profile design success could not be questioned.

Merchandising

Lagerfeld's approach to the established fashion conventions has been applied to a wide range of the Chanel merchandise, such as the heavy low-slung leather thonged chain belts. Similarly, bold costume accessories were added to his seriously smart suits – large "CC" logoed earrings, huge fake pearls, several gold chains, and gold medallions hung with discs, or sometimes even a Chanel nameplate. As Coco Chanel had dictated what was fashionable and what was not in her time, so too did Karl Lagerfeld in his. Both were prepared to shock the fashion world with their pioneering styles and designs and their focus on accessories.

The Chanel name became primarily about big business. The company was artfully promoted and commercialized into one of the most valuable brand names in the fashion and beauty industry. It became a hugely profitable international organization employing thousands of people in retailing and manufacturing. Apart from slight variations in some

"Lagerfeld's Chanel again looks modern, and smart women have adopted it as a basic classic. For an extraordinary number of smart women . . . a Chanel suit is the single most desirable fashion item of the mid-eighties."

Nicholas Coleridge,
from The Fashion Conspiracy.

of the sizes, the range of merchandise available didn't vary. Chanel shops all over the world projected the same image of expensive, seductive style, designed to appeal to the sophisticated woman of the world, rather than young minimal or wacky fashion tastes.

The famous perfumes, particularly Coco's classic No. 5, and No. 19, were prominently displayed in the extravagant-sized bottles created by Coco Chanel herself. Extensive and carefully coordinated ranges of top quality cosmetics, including special makeup kits with the latest body-care lotions, all carried the Chanel brand label. Trained staff offered customers individual advice on selecting beauty products and drew their attention to the wide selection of tempting accessories and clothes.

Costume jewels, patterned scarves, hats, decorated headbands, belts, and footwear were specially designed to go with the clothes. The aim was to complete Karl Lagerfeld's "look of the season" and encourage more purchases.

Fashion critics cast their expert eyes over the latest styles being paraded in front of them at a 1993 fashion show. The designer's work is finished – now it is up to the critics and the public to decide whether the designs will be a success.

The affluent customer could be body-prepared, made up, and dressed from head to toe in Chanel. If she felt generous, she could also find gifts for the man in her life since most boutiques carried a Chanel range of men's ties and colognes.

Making it

Coco Chanel learned her craft through traditional sewing and dressmaking which, with financial backing, led her to designing for individual clients. Her phenomenal success in this sphere introduced

The fashions of the 1990s reflect Coco Chanel's original designs from the early 1900s – even in the more unusual materials available to designers.

her to the world of the rich and famous and brought many opportunities into her business and private life.

Fashion developed in many directions during and after the influence of Coco Chanel. It expanded into a complex international industry. Technology became far more important. In the 1990s a potential designer, looking for recognition and financial success, had to be professionally trained in the basic principles of designing contemporary clothing. He or she had to learn about the content, performance and use of a vast range of fabrics, understanding how garments were cut and made with the latest machinery. It was important to learn how to design clothes that were suitable for manufacturing processes used at the time. The end products had to be acceptable to the highly competitive retail markets.

At the same time, like Coco, they had to possess a unique creative talent, great strength of character, and a determination to succeed.

The Chanel legacy

More than twenty years after her death the Chanel legend lived on and continued to be one of the most fascinating stories of the century. Newspapers, magazines, and books regularly quoted her views on fashion, individual stylishness, relationships, and women's role in life.

Her worldly wise attitudes were those of an intuitive French woman who strove to overcome a disadvantaged, poverty-stricken childhood. She worked, planned, and fought for her success in a male-dominated society.

Chanel used her appearance to help her. At a time when fashionable women were flamboyantly overdressed in a particularly feminine way, she adopted her own appealing, deceptively simple and practical style of dress. In doing so, she laid out the blueprint for the future of women's clothing.

Coco Chanel, born into a poor family in provincial France over a hundred years ago, had a profound effect on the way women dressed during her lifetime. Her influence has been firmly established to continue into the twenty-first century.